CHRISTMAS IN
NOTTINGHAM

Kipper Williams

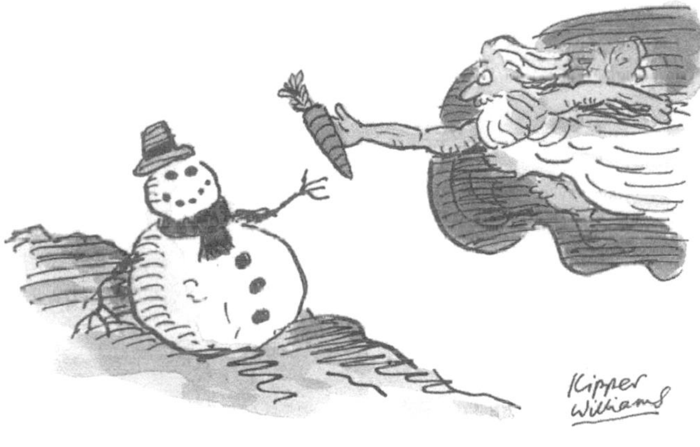
Kipper Williams

AMBERLEY

A number of these cartoons originally appeared in the Guardian, *the* Spectator, *the* Sunday Times, Private Eye, Country Life *or* Recharge, *so thanks to all concerned for allowing them to be used again here. Thanks also to* E&T *magazine for permission to reuse the cartoons on pages 4 and 14. Cartoons on pages 7, 15, 27 and 45 © Paperlink 2016.*

First published 2016

Amberley Publishing
The Hill, Stroud,
Gloucestershire, GL5 4EP
www.amberley-books.com

Copyright © Kipper Williams, 2016

The right of Kipper Williams to be identified
as the Author of this work has been asserted in
accordance with the Copyrights, Designs and
Patents Act 1988.

ISBN 978 1 4456 6368 5 (print)
ISBN 978 1 4456 6369 2 (ebook)

British Library Cataloguing in Publication Data.
A catalogue record for this book is available
from the British Library.

Typesetting and Origination by Amberley
Publishing.
Printed in the UK.

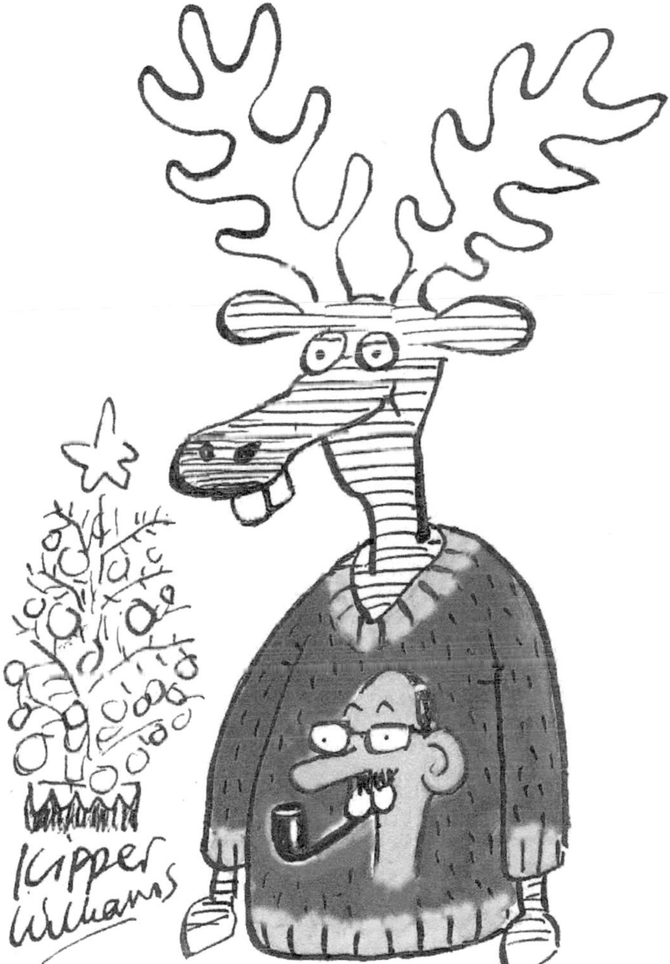
Kipper Williams

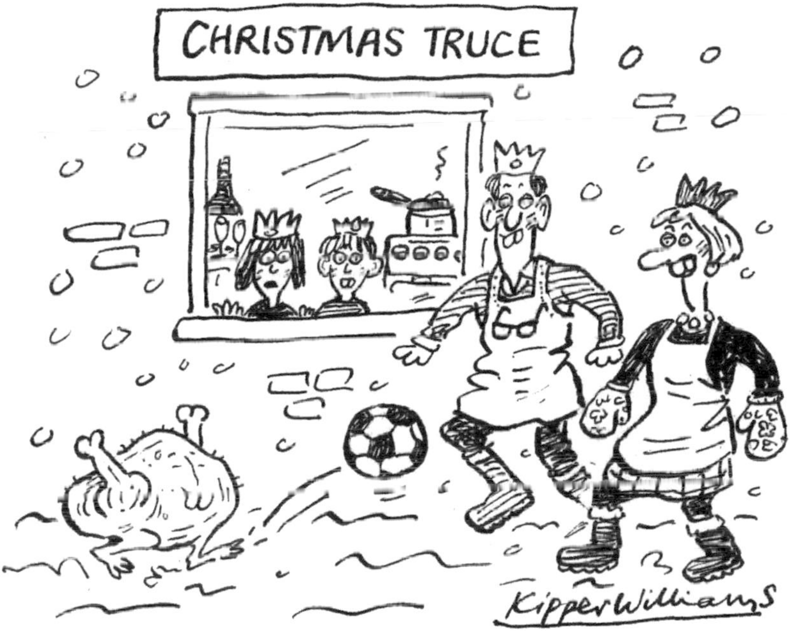
CHRISTMAS TRUCE
Kipper Williams

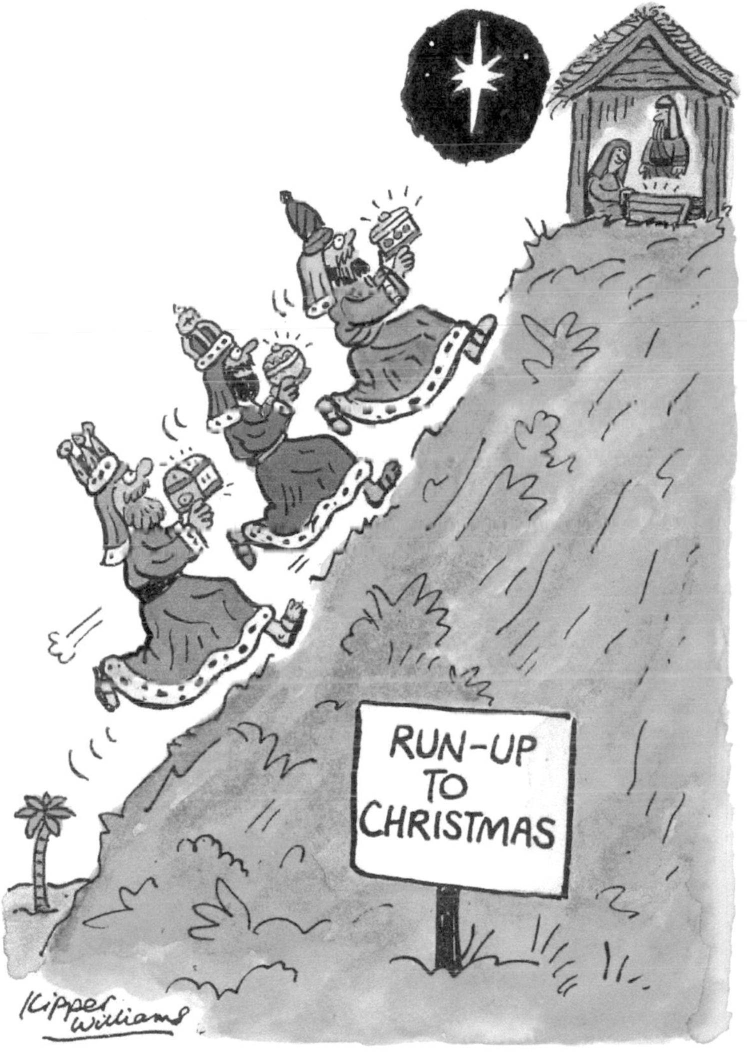
RUN-UP
TO
CHRISTMAS
Kipper Williams

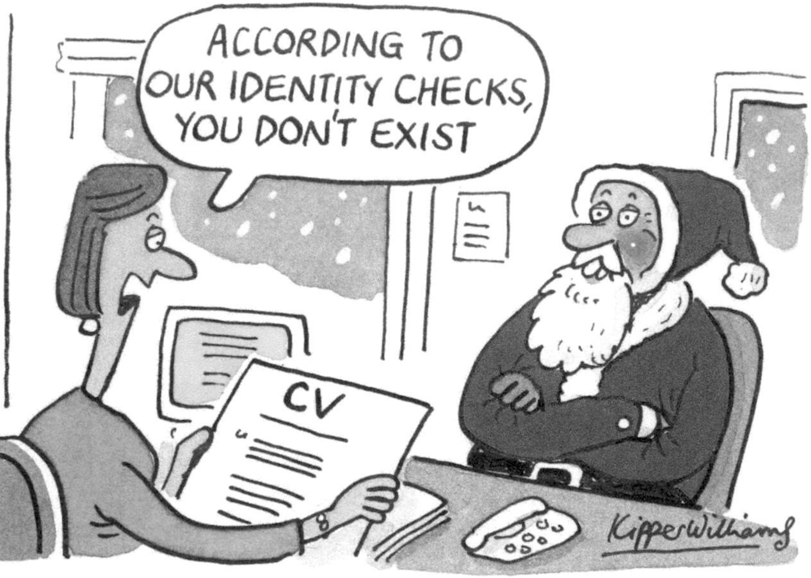
ACCORDING TO OUR IDENTITY CHECKS, YOU DON'T EXIST
CV
KipperWilliams

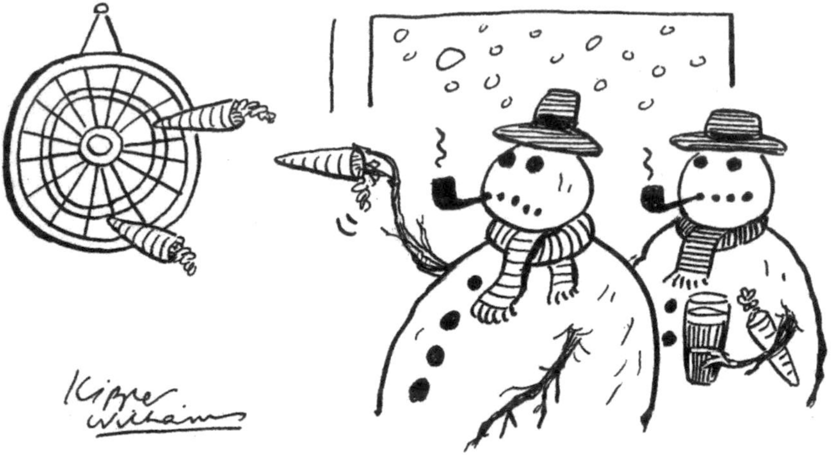
Kipper Williams

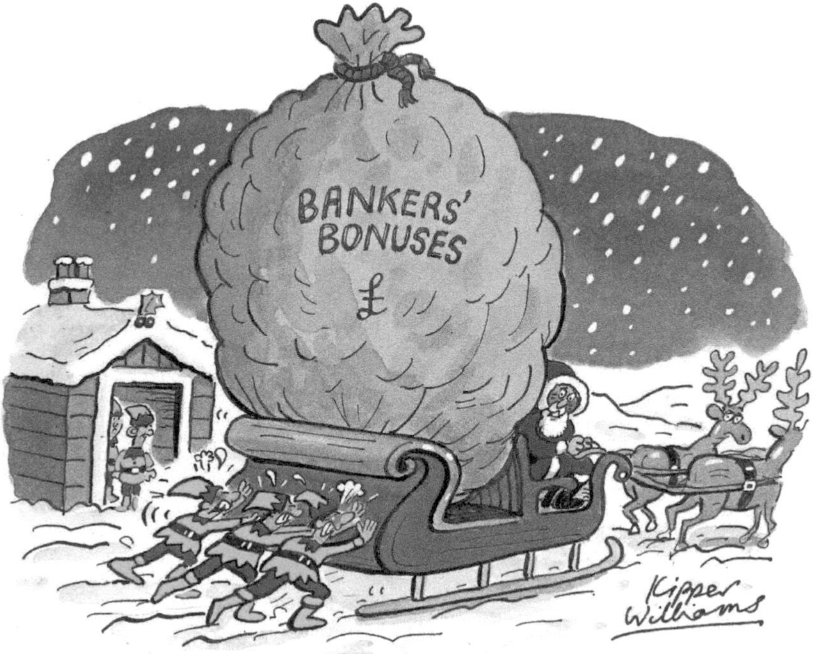
BANKERS' BONUSES
£
Kipper Williams

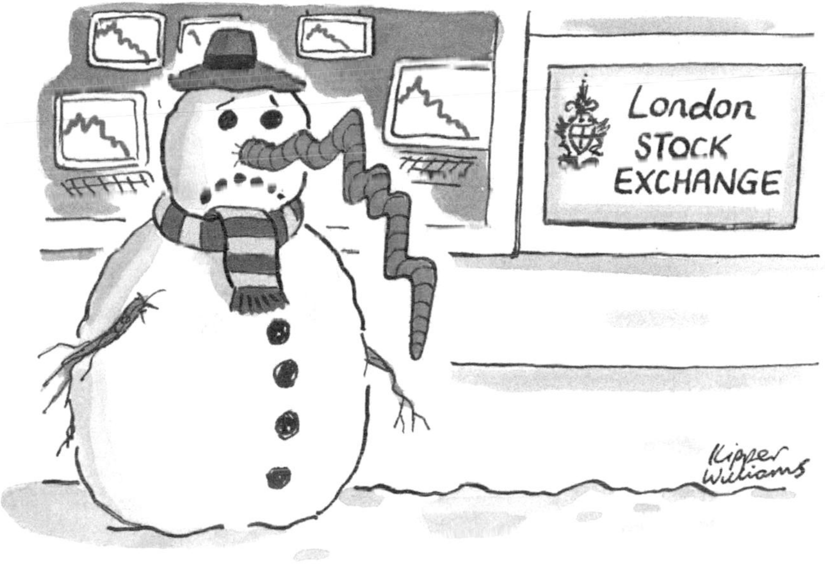
London
STOCK
EXCHANGE
Kipper Williams

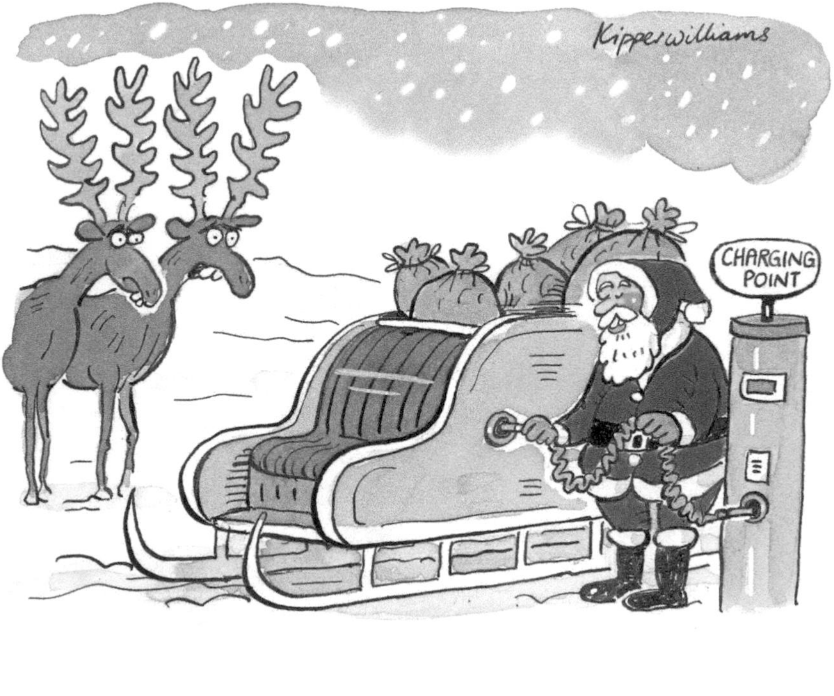
Kipperwilliams
CHARGING POINT

Kipper Williams

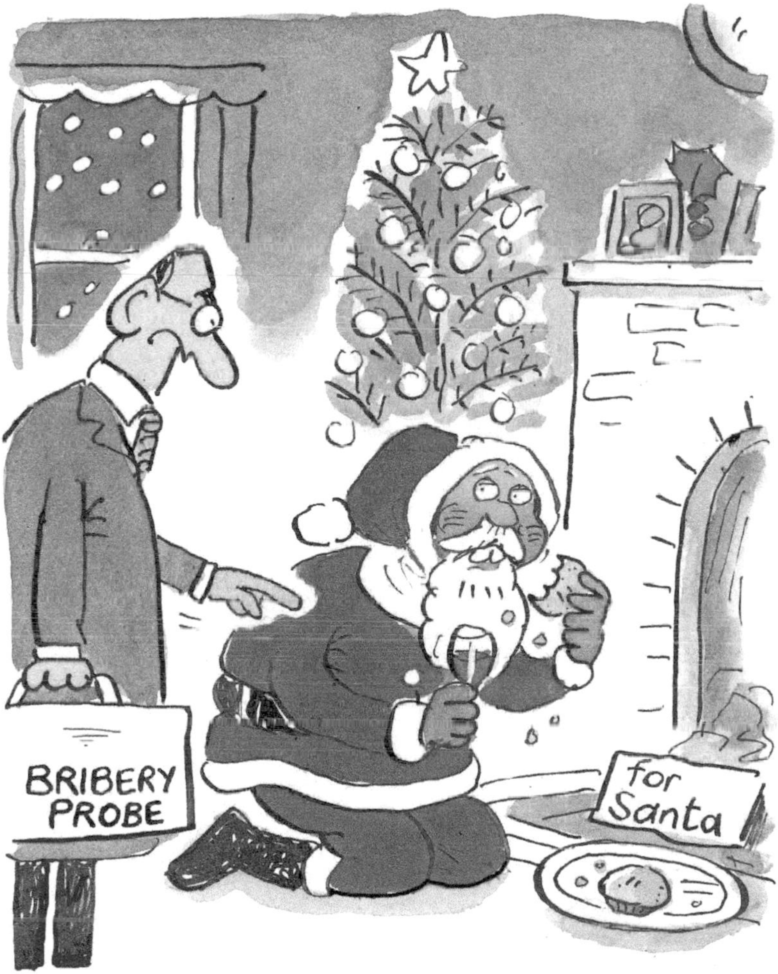
BRIBERY
PROBE
for
Santa

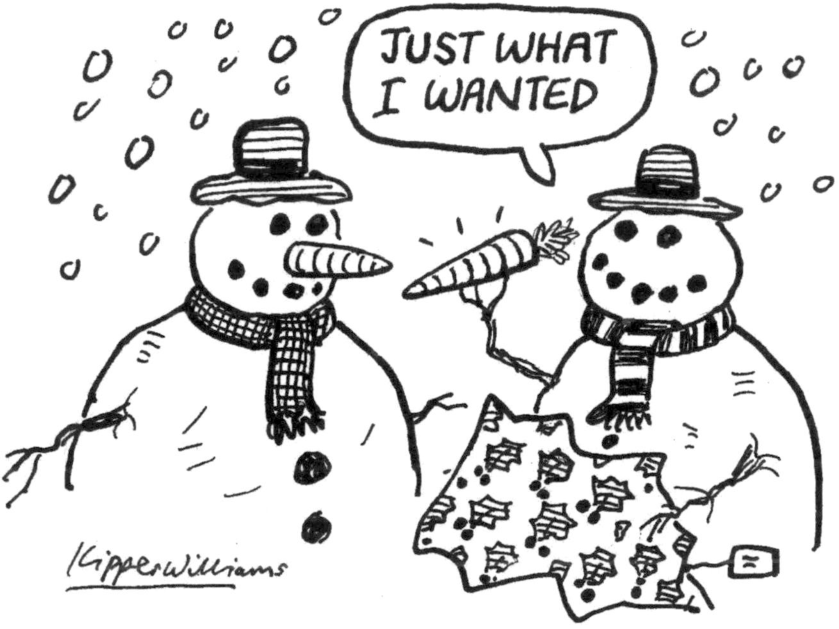
JUST WHAT I WANTED
Kipper Williams

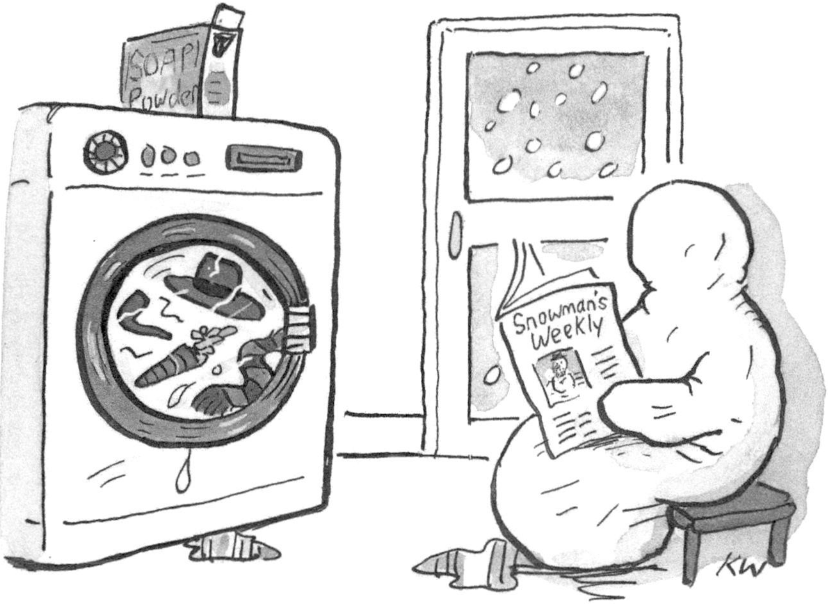

SOAP Powder
Snowman's Weekly
KW

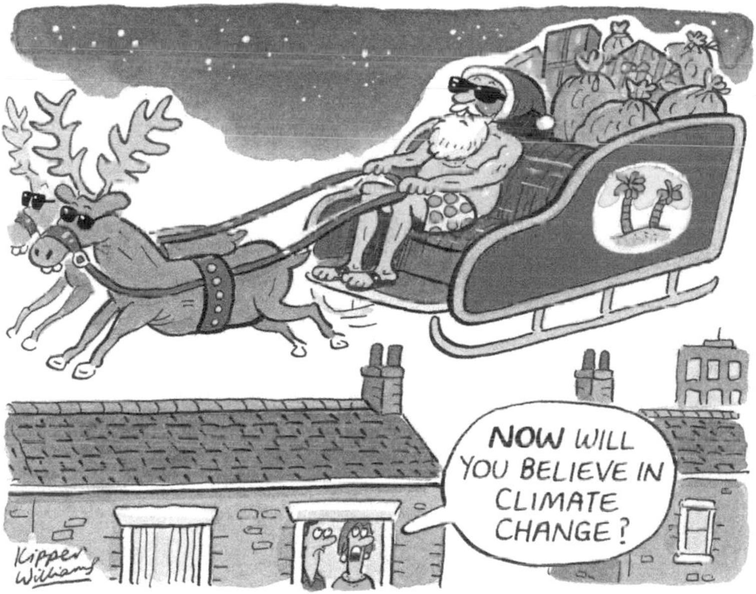
NOW WILL YOU BELIEVE IN CLIMATE CHANGE?
Kipper Williams

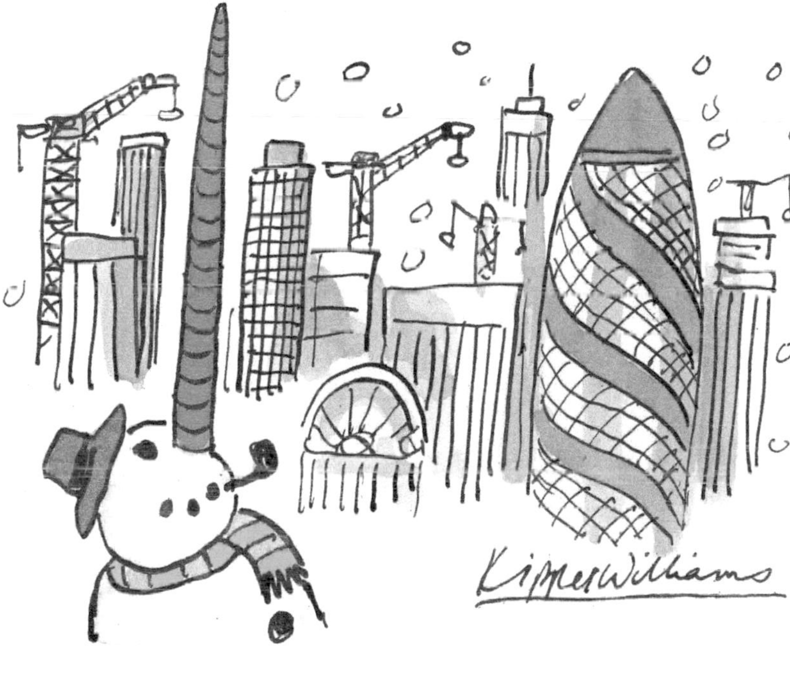
KipperWilliams

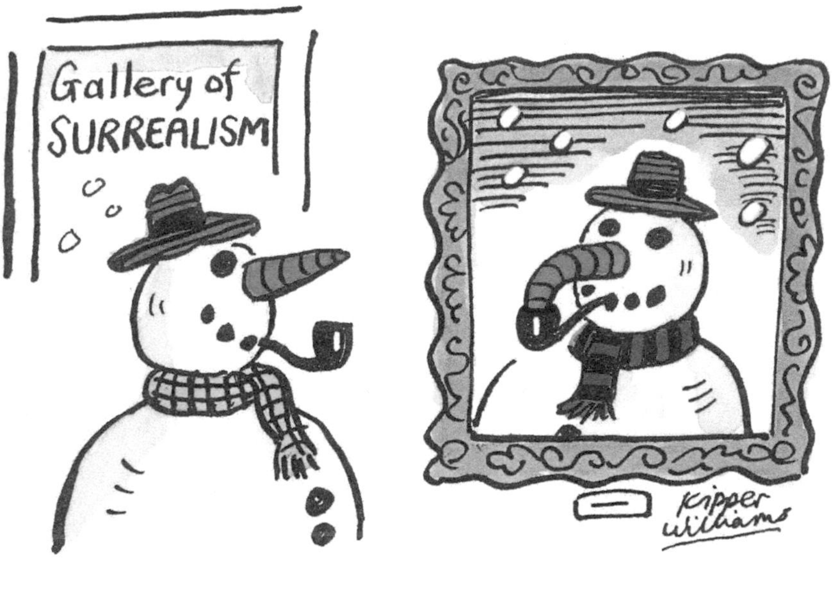
Gallery of
SURREALISM
kipper williams

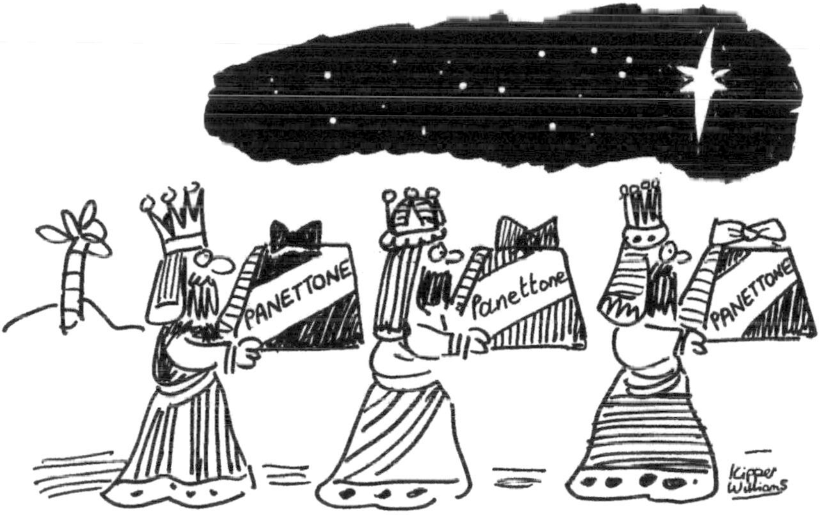
PANETTONE
Panettone
PANETTONE
Kipper Williams

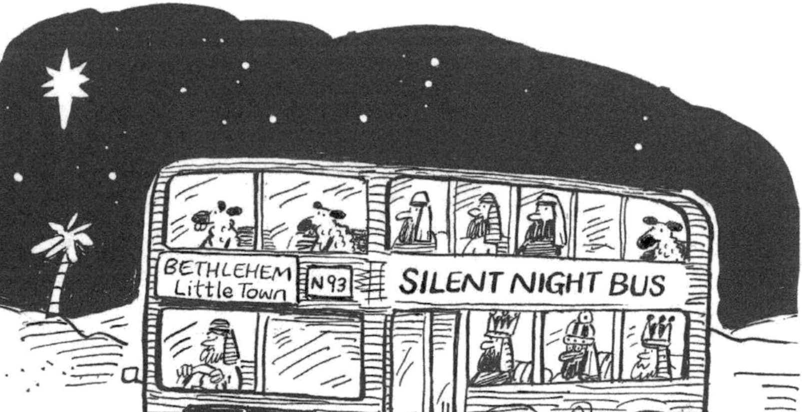
BETHLEHEM
Little Town
N93
SILENT NIGHT BUS
KipperWilliams

'Across the field, left at the fountain,
over the moor and right at the mountain.'

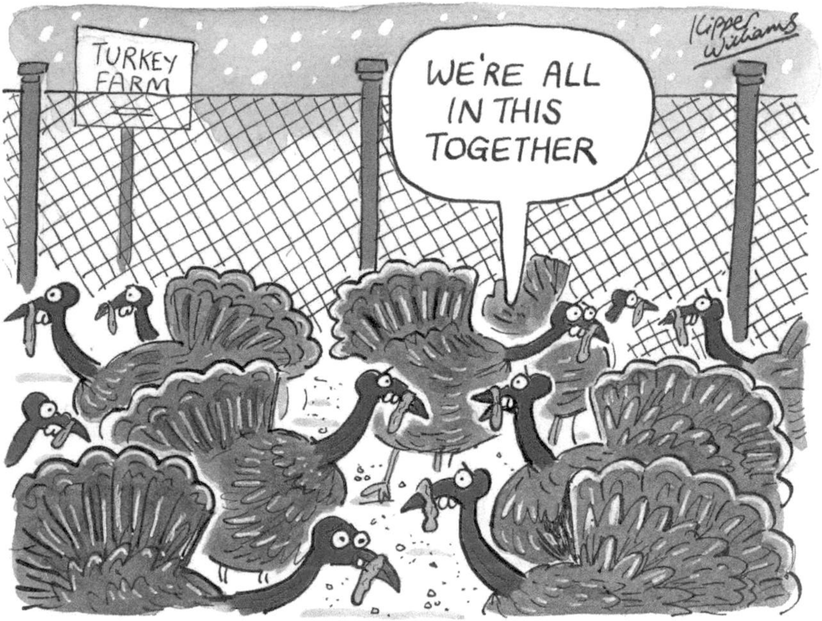
TURKEY FARM
WE'RE ALL IN THIS TOGETHER
Kipper Williams

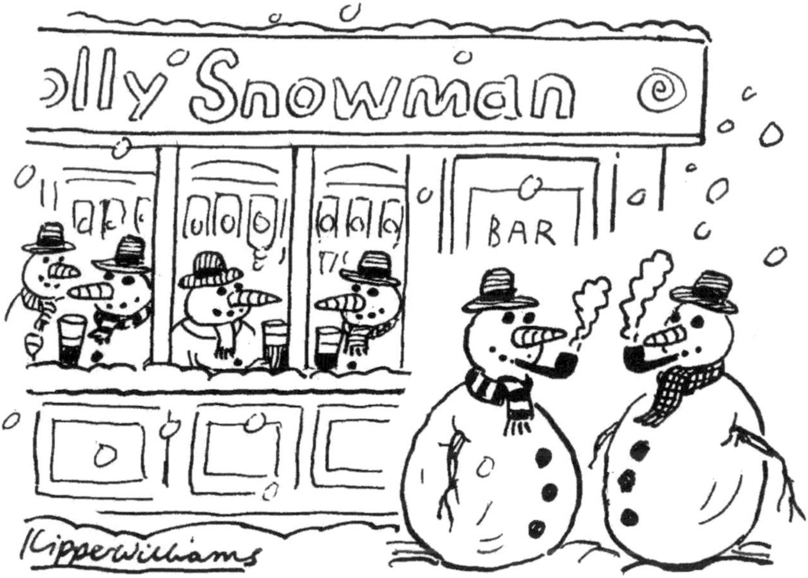
olly Snowman
BAR
KipperWilliams

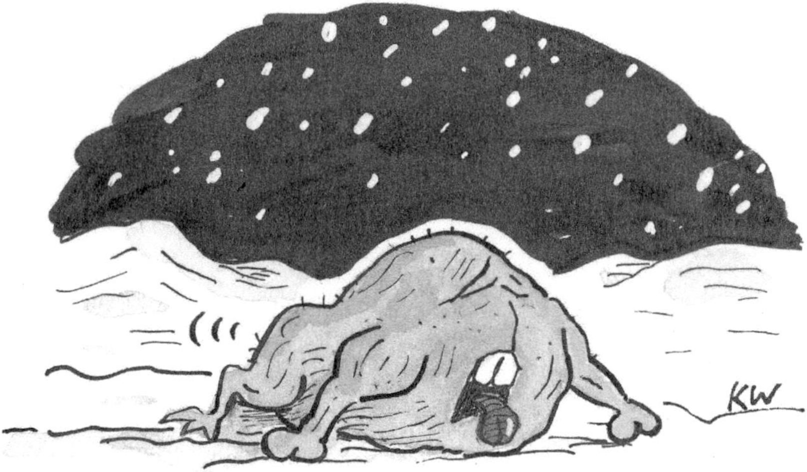
KW

'Stuffing . . . stuffing . . .'

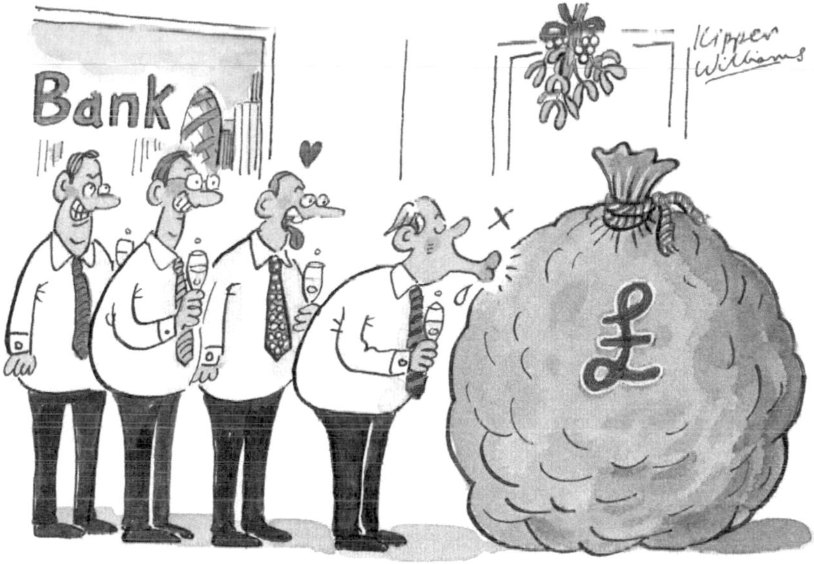
Bank
Kipper Williams

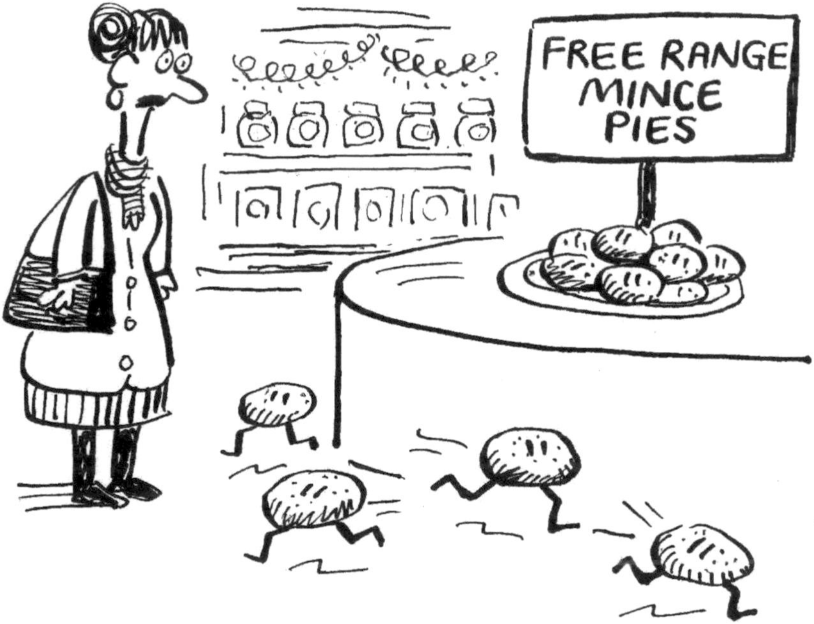
FREE RANGE
MINCE
PIES

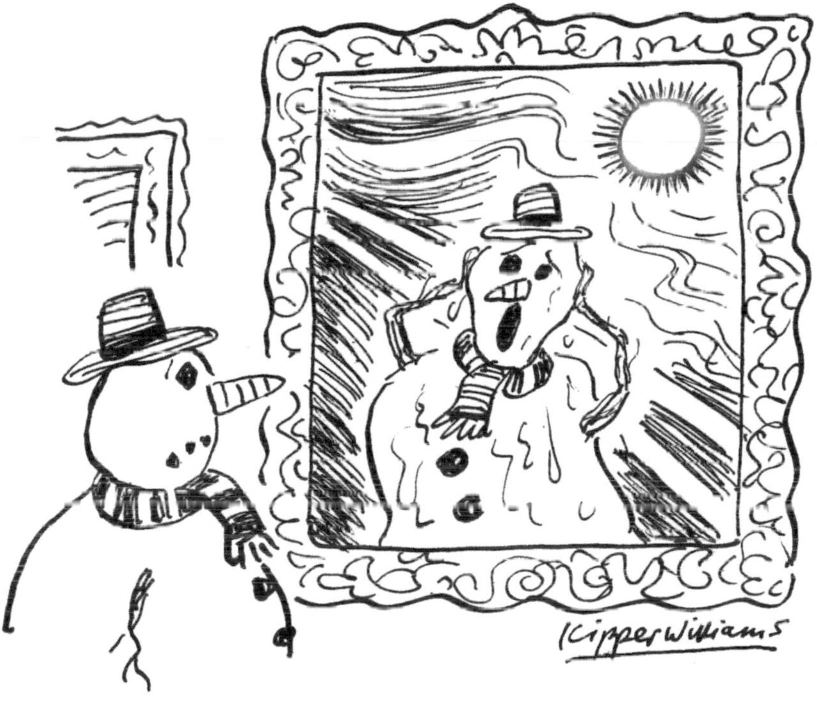
Kipper Williams

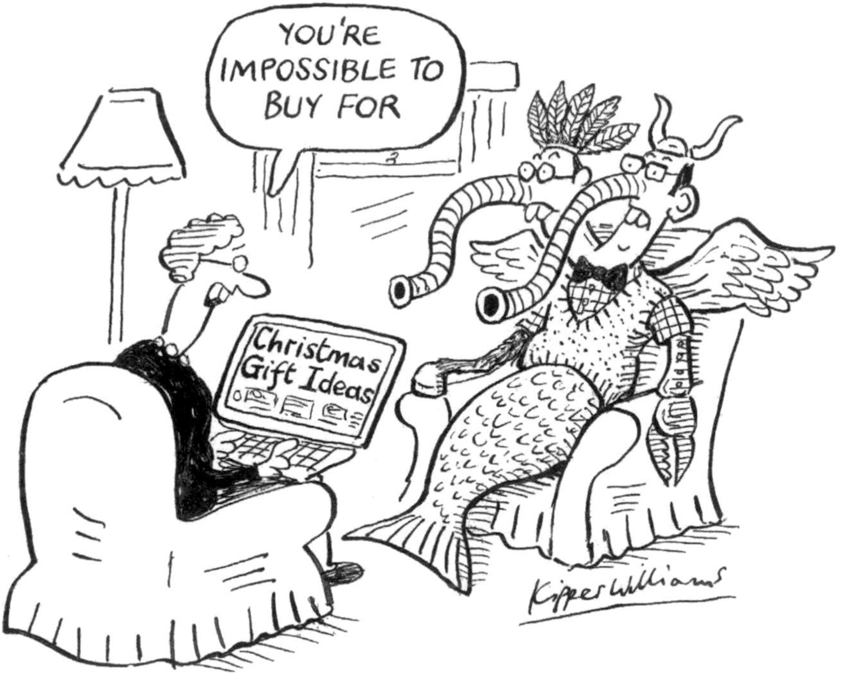
YOU'RE IMPOSSIBLE TO BUY FOR
Christmas Gift Ideas
Kipper Williams

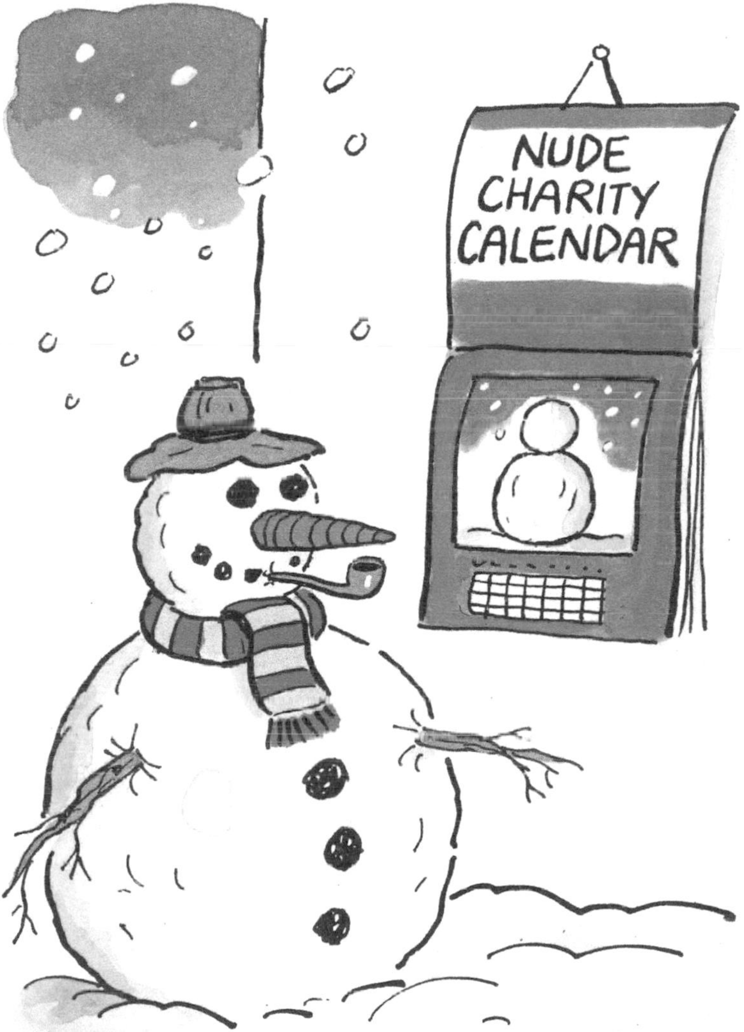
NUDE CHARITY CALENDAR
Kipper Williams

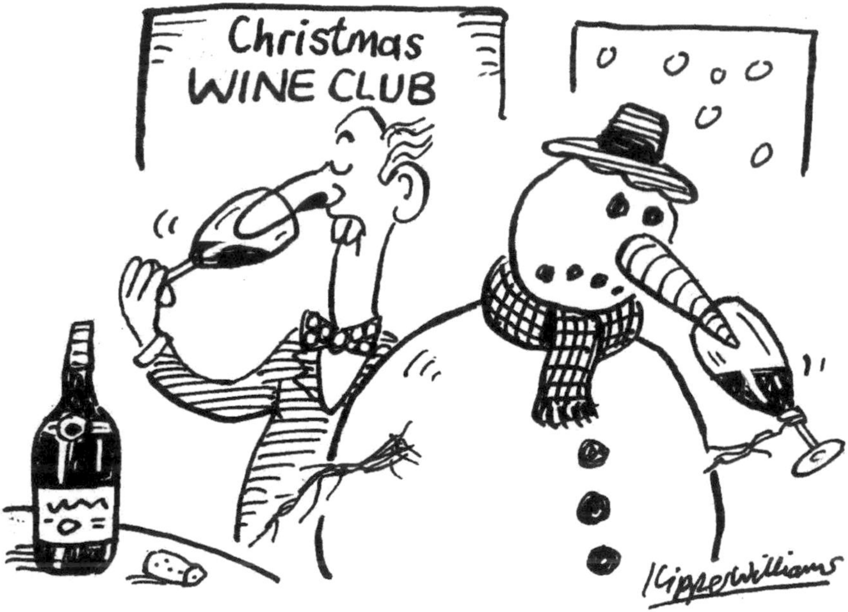
Christmas
WINE CLUB
KipperWilliams

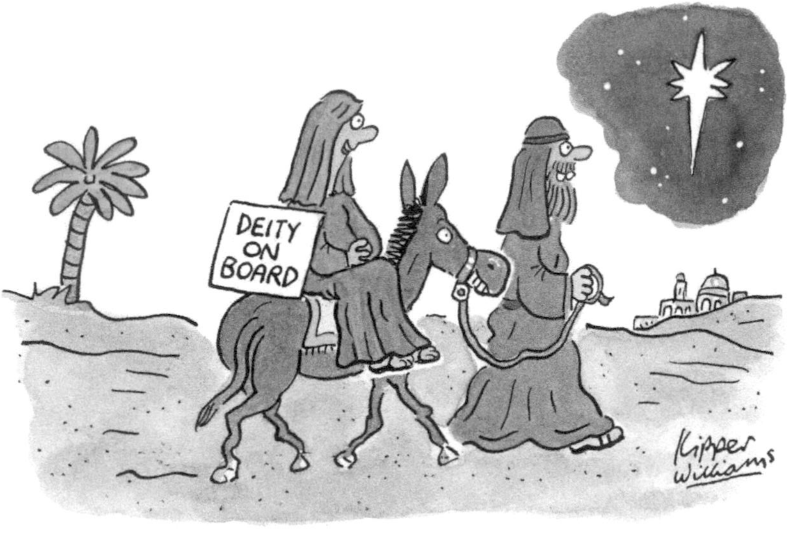
DEITY
ON
BOARD
Kipper
Williams

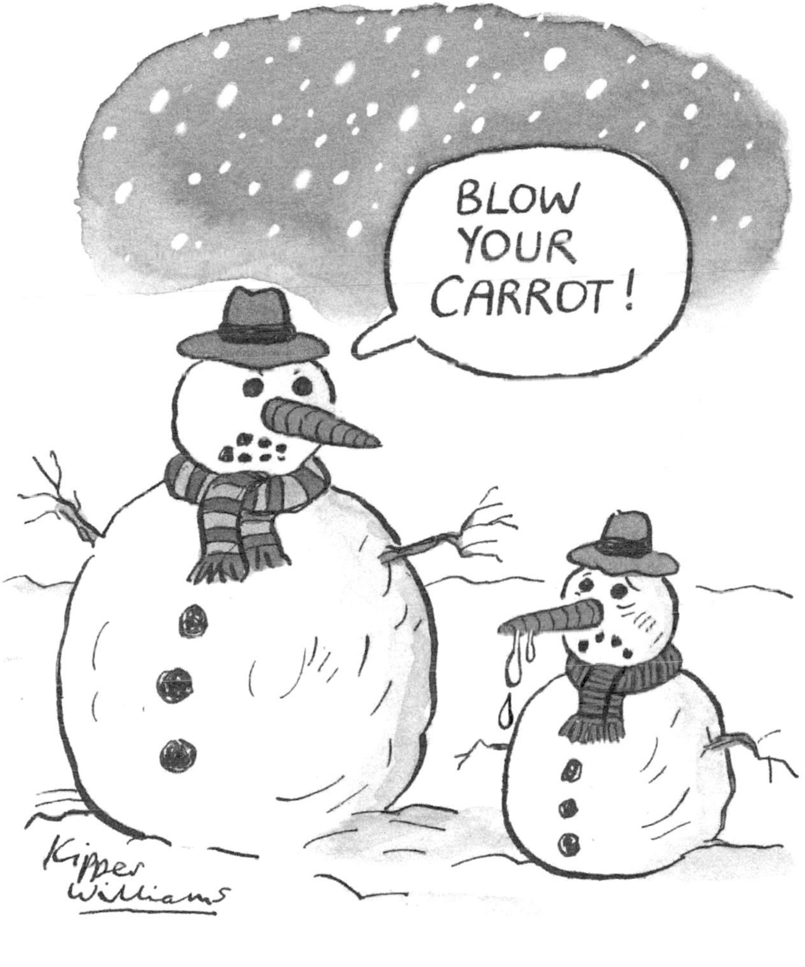
BLOW YOUR CARROT!
Kipper Williams

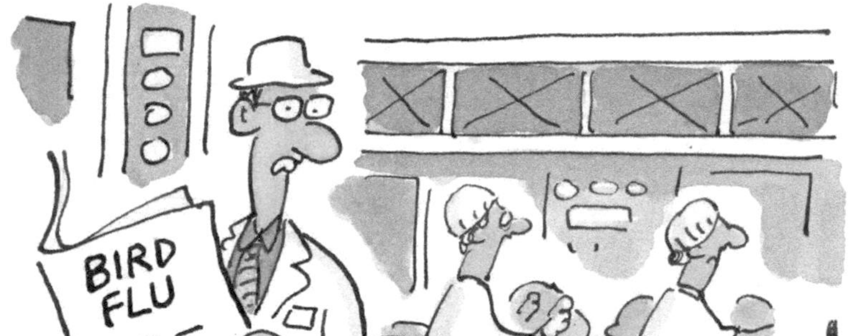
BIRD FLU
ACHOO!

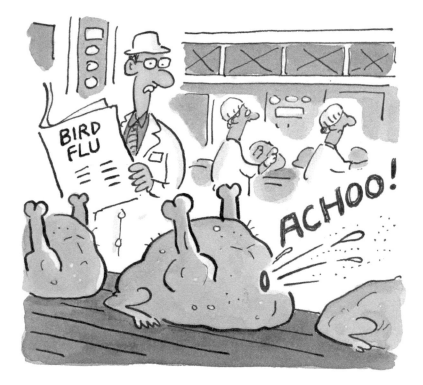

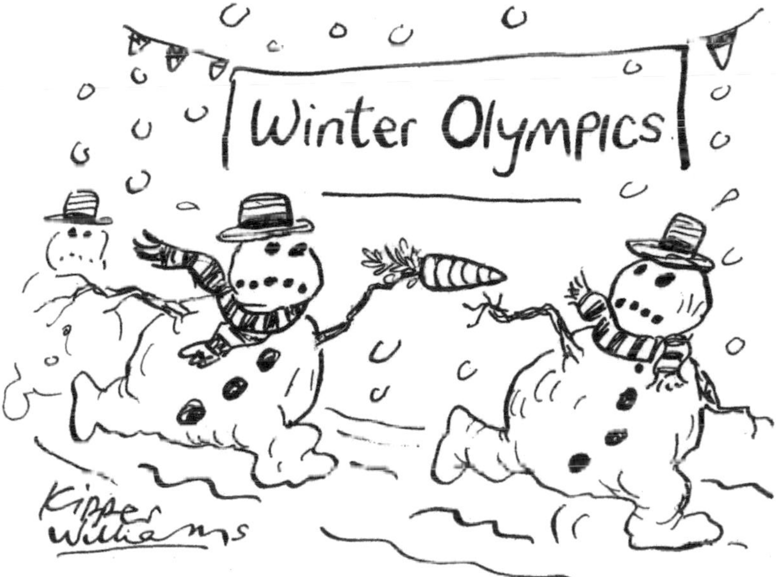
Winter Olympics
Kipper Williams

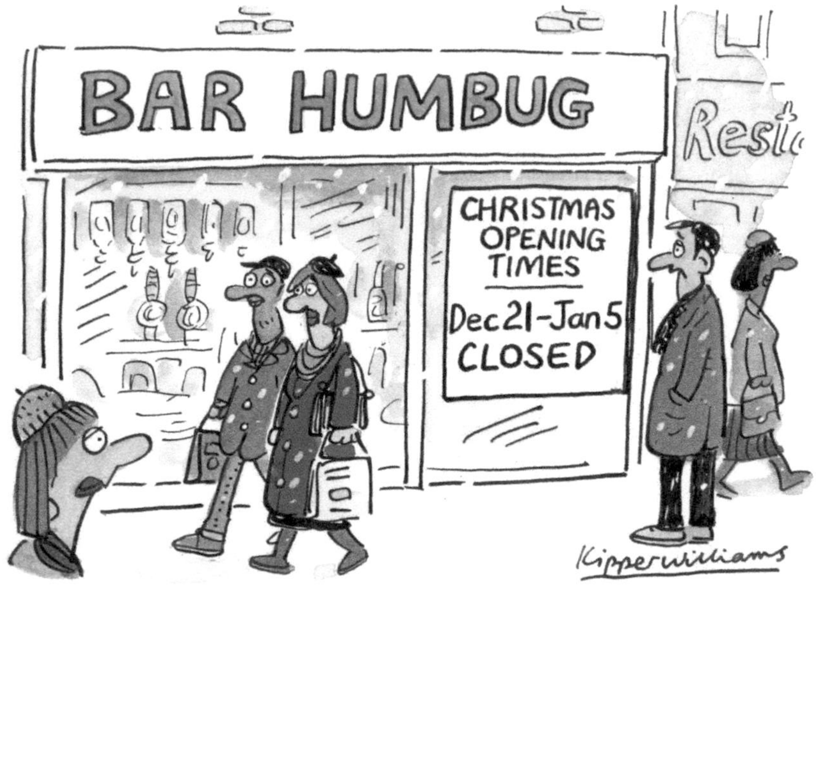
BAR HUMBUG
Resi
CHRISTMAS
OPENING
TIMES
Dec 21-Jan 5
CLOSED
KipperWilliams

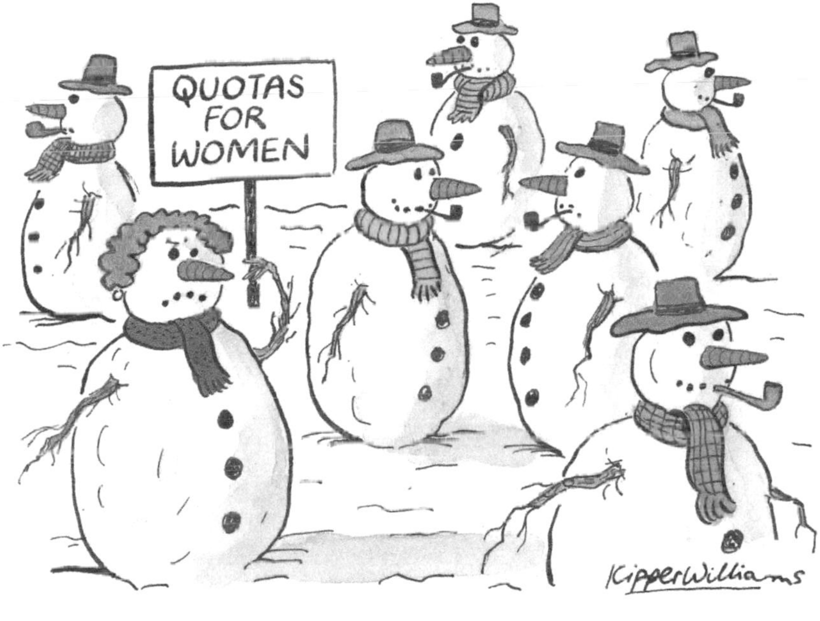
QUOTAS FOR WOMEN
KipperWilliams

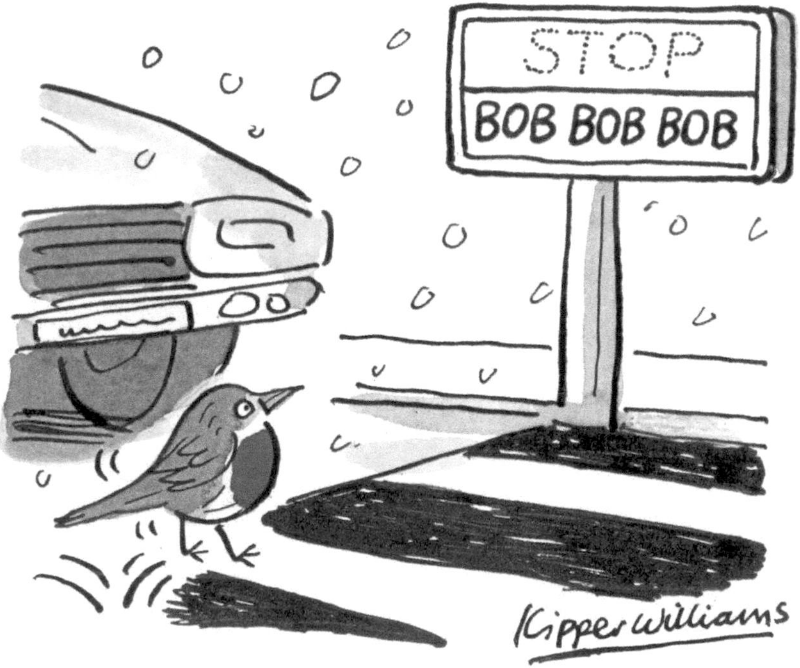
STOP
BOB BOB BOB
Kipper Williams

'This year I'll be heading somewhere hot.'

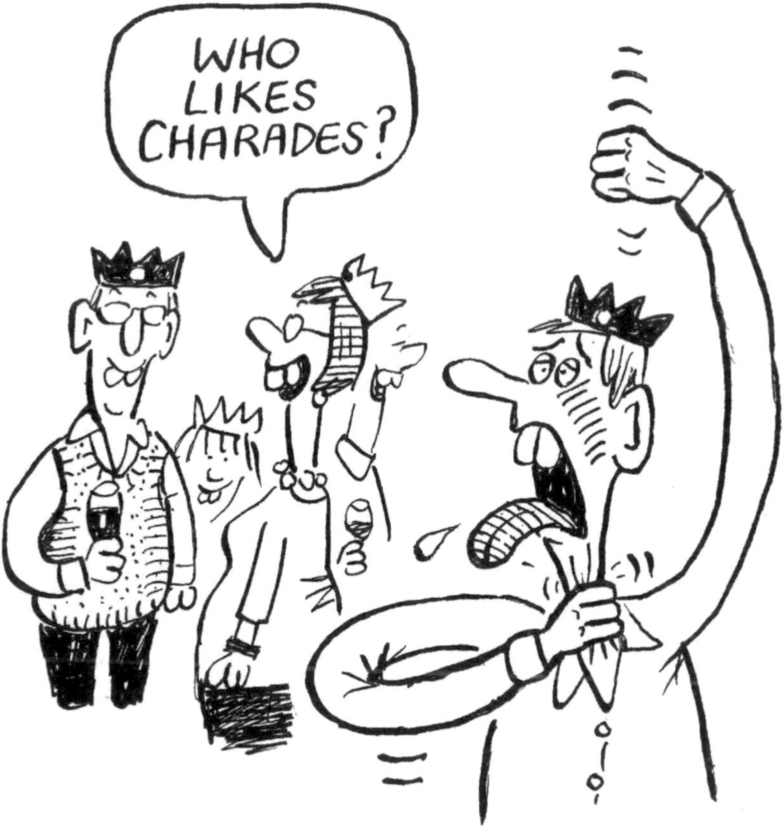
WHO LIKES CHARADES?

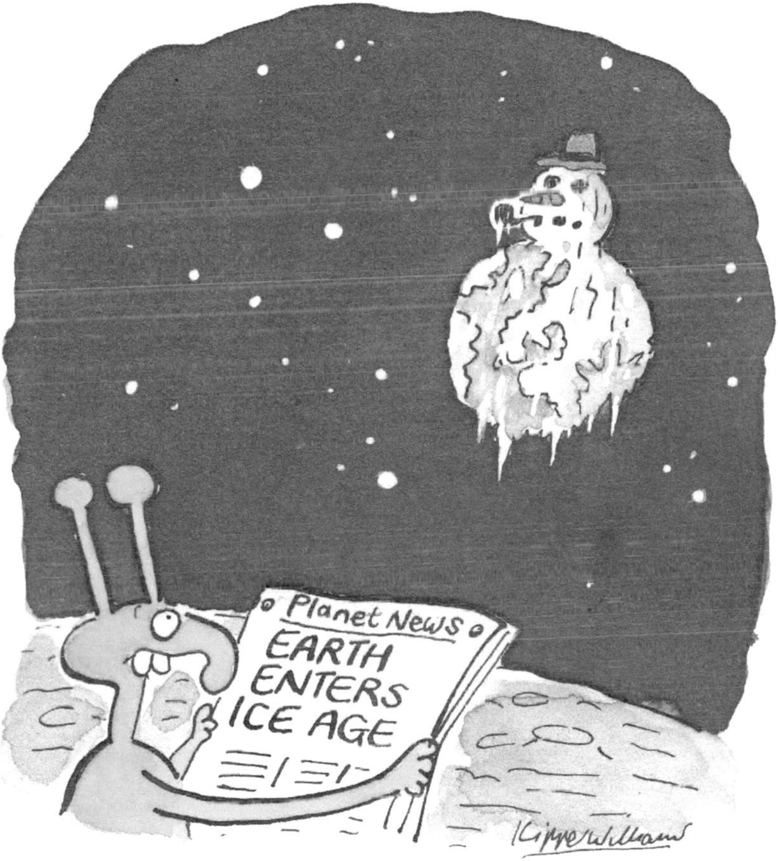
Planet News
EARTH ENTERS ICE AGE
KipperWilliams

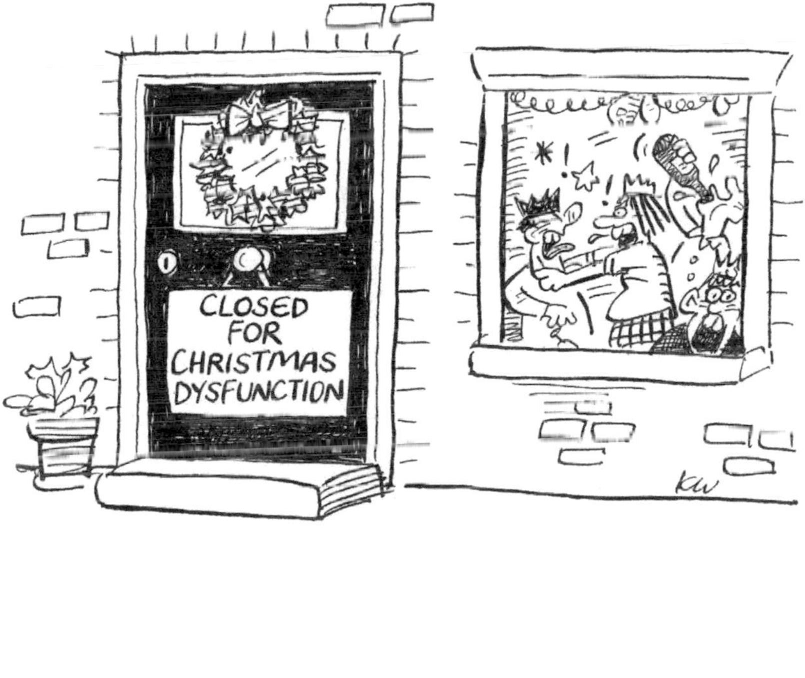
CLOSED
FOR
CHRISTMAS
DYSFUNCTION
KW

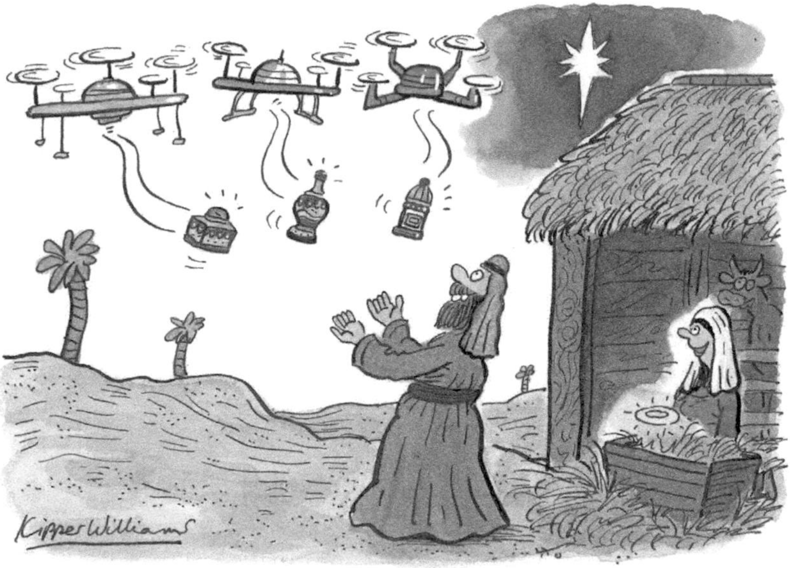
Kipper Williams

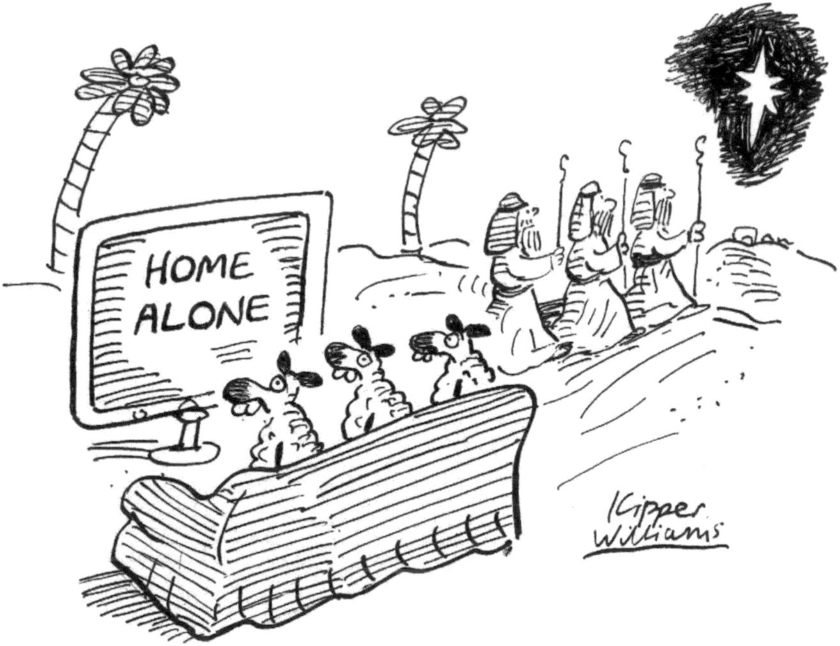
HOME
ALONE
Kipper
Williams

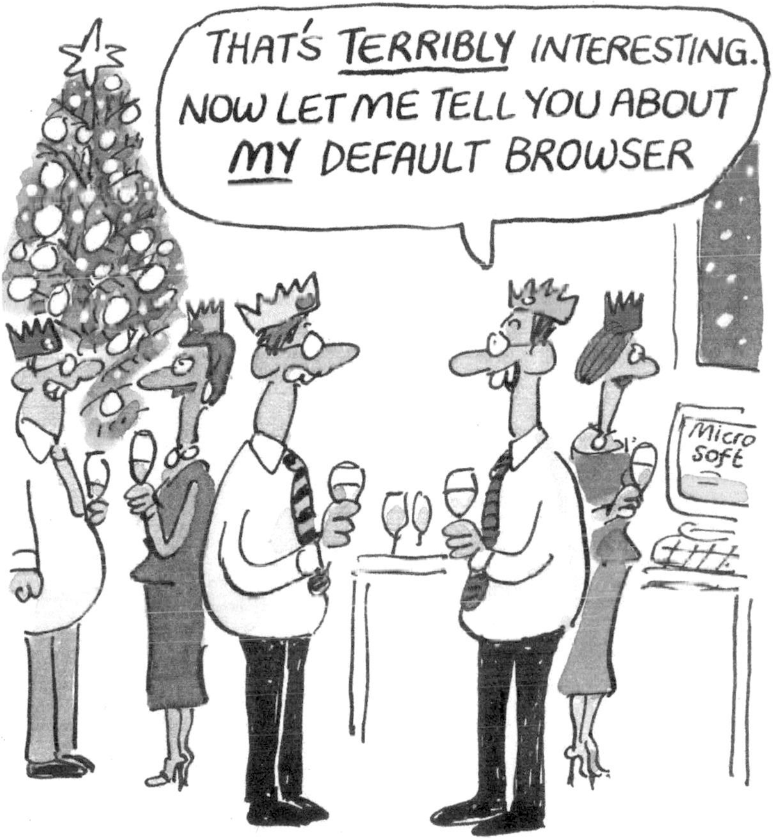
THAT'S TERRIBLY INTERESTING. NOW LET ME TELL YOU ABOUT MY DEFAULT BROWSER
Micro Soft

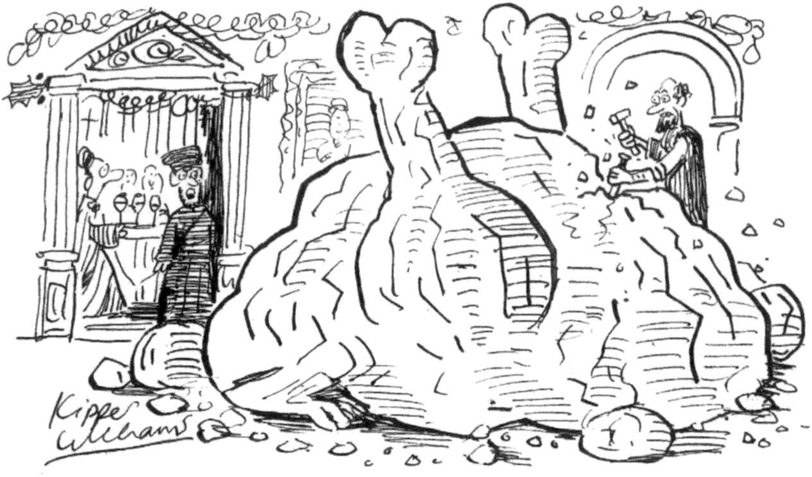
Kipper Williams

'Michelangelo, when I asked you to carve...'

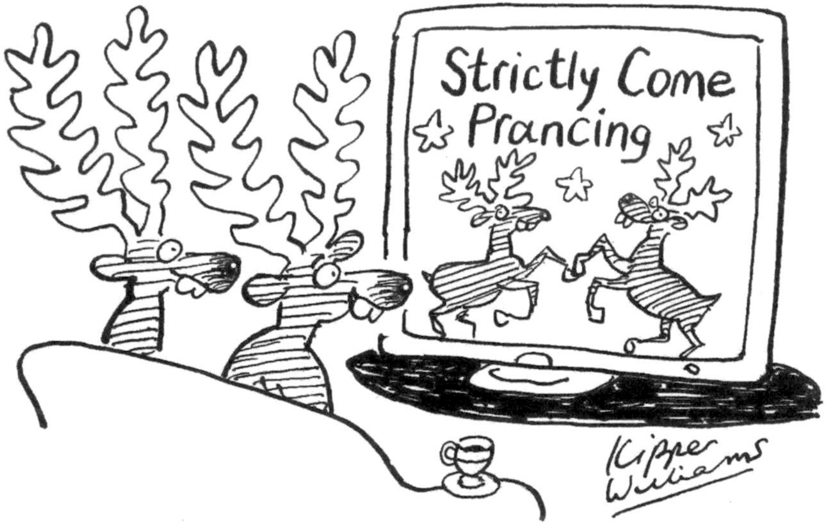
Strictly Come Prancing
Kipper Williams

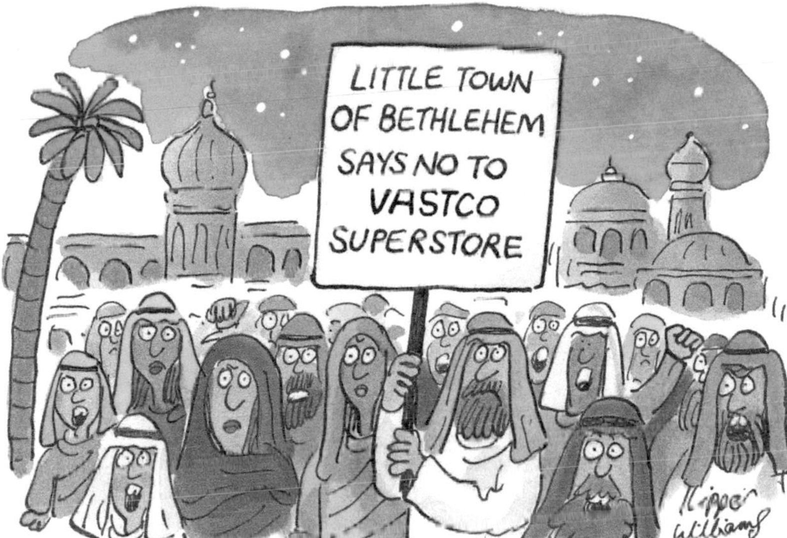
LITTLE TOWN OF BETHLEHEM SAYS NO TO VASTCO SUPERSTORE
Kipper Williams

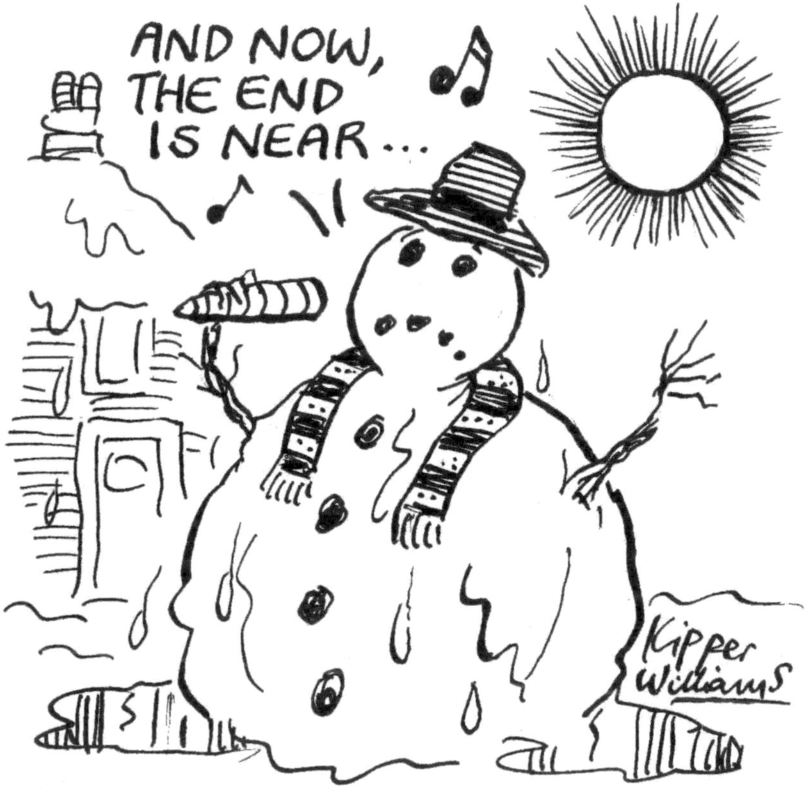
AND NOW, THE END IS NEAR...
Kipper Williams